Praise for WHAT WILL SOON TAKE PLACE

What Will Soon Take Place contains poems that live and move and have their being in the tension between the transcendent and the mundane—between the sharp pain of stepping on your kid's Lego block and the breathtaking awe attendant upon the Four Last Things. Tania Runyan's gift as a poet is to show us that the weight of our ultimate destiny lies hidden within the tedious chores and quiet joys of what we like to call "normal life." In that sense, this collection constitutes an "apocalypse"—a revelation—that is at once disturbing, comic, and ultimately consoling.

—GREGORY WOLFE, Editor of *Image* and author of *Beauty Will Save the World*

Have you ever wondered how the great book of Revelation, that final, apocalyptic book of the Bible, could possibly speak to our suburban American lives? In these poems the Third Horseman of the Apocalypse, the Sixth Seal, and The Whore of Babylon meet Jell-O, carpooling, and Hollywood. The effect is sometimes terrifying, sometimes funny, often moving, always thought-provoking.

—JEANNE MURRAY WALKER, author of *Helping the Morning: New and Selected Poems*

This bold collection is a stunning exercise in cohesion, the seaming together of the ragged edges of ancient visions with present-day human conflict. These poems reveal the visceral views of both the prophet and the writer. (Who can explicate the Revelation better than a poet?) Adept at free and formal verse, she surprises us with glints of pain and glory in every line, glimpses of a future revealed in symbols that seem to challenge her on every front. Tania Runyan does this like no one I know.

—LUCI SHAW, author of *Sea Glass: New and Selected Poems*, and Writer in Residence, Regent College

The book of Revelation was not one of Martin Luther's favorites, but that is because he had not read Tania Runyan's piercing interpretations of it, poems which "enter through the garage instead," revealing Jesus in the ordinary and everyday, as we do what we do—driving the expressway, going on business trips, shopping at Old Navy, waiting at the drive-through. The silence in heaven at a writers' retreat, the antichrist at the mall, a poetry reading feat ___ ___ these poems the last things are familiar imag ___ aordinary visions of the Spirit-infused uni ___ In poems of trenchant beauty Tania Runy ___ vision and reveals the utterly real world of ___

—JILL BAUMGAERTNER, Poetry Editor of *The Christian* ___ ___ ___thor of four poetry collections, including *What Cannot Be Fixed* (Cascade Books, 2014)

WHAT WILL SOON TAKE PLACE

POEMS

TANIA RUNYAN

PARACLETE PRESS
BREWSTER, MASSACHUSETTS

2017 First Printing

What Will Soon Take Place: Poems

Copyright © 2018 by Tania Runyan

All rights reserved.

ISBN 978-1-61261-857-9

The Paraclete Press name and logo (dove on cross) are trademarks of Paraclete Press, Inc.

Library of Congress Cataloging-in-Publication Data
Names: Runyan, Tania, author.
Title: What will soon take place : poems / by Tania Runyan.
Description: Brewster, Massachusetts : Paraclete Press, [2017]
Identifiers: LCCN 2017040952 | ISBN 9781612618579 (trade paper)
Classification: LCC PS3618.U5668 A6 2017 | DDC 811/.6— dc23
LC record available at https://lccn.loc.gov/2017040952

10 9 8 7 6 5 4 3 2 1

Published by Paraclete Press
Brewster, Massachusetts
www.paracletepress.com

Printed in the United States of America

for my ragged band

CONTENTS

LOCUSTS ON THE EARTH

AND
THEY
SANG
A
NEW
SONG

FOREWORD

The summer after my freshman year of high school, I came face to face with Jesus Christ while watching the *Phil Donahue Show*.

I'd been lying on the floor of my sister's living room on a blistering June day in southern California's Inland Empire. The silver-haired talk show host had invited Elizabeth Clare Prophet, founder of a cult known as the Church Universal and Triumphant, to speak about an impending nuclear attack (from Russia, of course) that would herald the end of the world.

Suddenly, I started shaking and crying. I wanted to run, but my bare feet had nowhere to land but the hot asphalt of Del Norte Place simmering under a blanket of smog. I looked out the window, suddenly despondent for the semi trucks that rumbled over the 60 freeway oblivious to their imminent destruction.

"Why are you afraid?" my sister, fourteen years my senior, asked.

"What do you think will happen to you when the world ends?"

I told her I hadn't thought about the world ending. While I felt personally invincible, like most teenagers, I hadn't considered that the planet could go first.

She told me that Jesus had died for my sins so that when I die—or the world blows up, whichever comes first—I would go to heaven. All I had to do was pray to receive the gift, no rules or rituals required. I had never heard of this approach to God. Or, perhaps, if I had, I hadn't understood or paid attention.

"I guess I do feel like something's missing from my life," I hiccupped and sniffed.

My sister quoted *Revelation*: "Jesus said, 'I stand at the door and knock.'" Didn't I know that my terror and tears were Jesus' hand on the brass knocker, waking me from my sleep? How could I leave him standing out there? Of course I should open it, which in this case meant "receiving Jesus" by repeating a prayer my sister led. I didn't quite understand what was happening, but I knew it marked a change.

Years later, I would learn that this text (Rev. 3:20)—in fact, all of *Revelation*—was written to the existing church, not unbelievers. But during that afternoon in my sister's living room, the words worked for me, supplemented by a cult leader with feathered hair. With God, all things are possible.

For the next several years, I'd hear about the impending rapture and its false alarms, such as Harold Camping's ever-changing predictions in the early 90s and 2011, Heaven's Gate's Hale-Bopp scare of 1997, Nostradamus's foretellings, and a whole spate of millennial catastrophes—in a word, "what will soon take place" (Rev. 1:1). Evangelical Christians would come of age consuming *A Thief in the Night* and *Left Behind*, convinced that in case of rapture, their car would hurtle down the freeway unmanned.

Since then, I have changed in my theology. I'm no longer "pre-trib" or even premillennial, as I can't find enough biblical evidence to support those beliefs. Of course, these are not the doctrinal hills I choose to die on. There is too much trouble for today, as Jesus says, to argue about what's going to happen tomorrow. Following the Great Commandment feels demanding enough.

But then what is *Revelation* for?

Nearly three decades after my talk show conversion, I still hadn't read *Revelation* all the way through. It was a confusing, violent book that seemed to have nothing to do with the compassionate Jesus I'd learned to trust. I hated how the book's garish, terrifying imagery had been used to scare people into Christianity–even though my own faith had been sown in fear.

But the passage that had spoken to me in the midst of my fear that summer afternoon is, indeed, from *Revelation*. And a scene that would later comfort me through the many anxieties of my youth—a fiery, sword-mouthed, waterfall-voiced Jesus who reaches out to John and says, "Do not be afraid"—hails from *Revelation* as well. Bits and pieces of this letter to the seven churches would haunt me with its tensions of love and terror, and the image of the Messiah who blasted the universe from a star, healing humans with a fleshly touch.

I had to face a question: If I was too scared to read a book of the New Testament (don't even get me started on the Old), how strong was my faith? If *Revelation* had nothing to say to me, what did that indicate about Scripture in general, or at least my view of it? Was Jesus paging through the Bible, shaking his head, and saying in the voice of Ron Howard on *Arrested Development*, "They made a huge mistake"?

It was time to gather some resources, which, when it comes to *Revelation*, can be an infuriating task. I'm no biblical scholar, so I tend to search for books geared toward decently read lay people. Not surprisingly, volumes of flame-covered, politically fraught propaganda books filled my search results for commentaries. Then I found Ed Cyzewski and Larry Helyer's *The Good News of Revelation*. Good news? When are sulfur-breathing locusts with bad hairstyles good news?

As Cyzewski and Helyer emphasize from the get-go, John wrote *Revelation* to comfort the suffering early church, not stir us into a twenty-first-century tizzy about which world leaders will play the parts of dragons and whores. Reading *Revelation* through the seven churches' eyes helped me to understand the intent behind John's book, which he wrote to communicate the hope and beauty of Christ's victory over hopelessness and suffering. His enduring love. The Alpha and Omeganess of it all.

By reading *Revelation* in the context of the past rather than the future, I live it more fully in the present. Revelation isn't about preparing for tomorrow's apocalypse, but clinging to God today, drawing near to him amidst dangers, whether they come from outside violence, personal doubt, or his own terrifying love that simply won't take lukewarm for an answer.

In writing these poems, I've drawn closer to the mysteries of *Revelation* rather than formulating answers, predictions, or theories. I no longer want to run from *Revelation*, but toward it, even when it scares and offends me. In the middle of all those beasts, gemstones, eyes, and swords, I listen for the knock. I hope these poems might beckon you to a deeper listening as well.

Revelation isn't about preparing for tomorrow's apocalypse, but clinging to God today, drawing near to him amidst dangers, whether they come from outside violence, personal doubt, or his own terrifying love that simply won't take lukewarm for an answer.

In writing these poems, I've drawn closer to the mysteries of Revelation rather than formulating answers, predictions, or theories. I no longer want to run from Revelation, but toward it, even when it scares and offends me. In the middle of all those beasts, gemstones, eyes, and swords, I listen for the knock. I hope these poems might beckon you to a deeper listening as well.

—Tania Runyan

ANGEL
OVER
PATMOS

Patmos

No cave, cleft, or ocean shattering bluffs.
The only trumpet "Hot Cross Buns"

blatting from my daughter's open window.
I circle the block to find my messengers:

a whimpering beagle roped to a magnolia,
ear flipped inside out. Cracked rainbow pinwheels,

plaster Nessie in the dandelions, all bought
and positioned for some prophecy of beauty.

If only a forsythia opened by my bedroom window,
I would spend a week in resurrection. If only

a birdbath and bench for prayer. Or a cherub
on the front steps, concrete wings spread

over a basket of trailing lobelia. Who could hide
from that serene, carved smile? But we always enter

through the garage instead: crushed milk bottles,
mud-scabbed boots, jump ropes coiled

with shovels and bikes. They were never meant to lie
in our way. Like it or not, they speak.

The Angel over Patmos

Such a burden of beasts
and rainbows, sulfur and emeralds
leaking from his knapsack
as John hunches in a cave down there,
picking at a skeleton of fish.

The body resists exile.
Even the smallest burrowing mite
is enough to make John claw his skin,
saltwater stiffening his hair
like the driftwood he tries to burn.

Any sort of trance is impossible
to achieve when shifting on rocks,
the fabric of your robe sticking
in your crack. But with time,
the Spirit will come.

The angel doodles dragons
in the air. He circles like a plane on hold
and waits for the one twilight
John will sigh, lift his chapped hands,
and receive his words like wounds.

The Cave of Patmos

Blessed is the one who reads aloud
the words of this prophecy.

John reclined in a cave
and echoed to God

what he heard:
incense, famine, Gog and Magog

filtering through bats' wings
like the words I chanted

into a box fan as a child.
Hell-o-o-o? Hell-o-o-o?

Here I a-a-am. Or just
ah-ah-ah-h-h-h,

my diced voice all
I understood about prayer,

the bumps on my wind-blown skin
His replies. And John dreaming

my face in the limestone
as the angel told him to speak.

Things That Will Soon Take Place

Will not rush through your heart like ball lightning.
They will smolder under your skin as you wait

for your chalupa in the drive-through
or latch the dressing room door at Old Navy,

wanting nothing more than to pull a preshrunk T
over your head in peace. But you must steady yourself

on the purse hook, nauseated by the spirit
burying inside you like a tick. Soon you will see

seraph wings in the price tags,
hear trumpets in the vents. You will awaken

to asphalt poking your soles like swords of fire,
to the grocery bagger's billowing breath.

These things will not horse through you
but nudge you like a dog in the street,

a matted earthbound begging for your touch,
wet nose you'll never wipe off.

Behold, He Is Coming on the Clouds

Jesus fishing for men in the mackerel sky.

Jesus shooting contrails from his wounds.

Jesus swinging in the low-slung hammock of a storm.

Jesus stratus boarding.

Jesus lobbing puffs of cumulonimbus at his enemies.

Jesus gripping a cirrus by its wispy reins and swooping down to the trees.

Jesus dissipating into fog and condensing on your glasses.

Jesus dampening your sleeve.

Jesus the smell of rain on your fingers.

Vision of the Son of Man

This morning I can't squeeze out
of my smallness. Damn the praise choirs
whining from my cell phone, the dot-to-dot
Jonahs crumpled in the back seat.
I want to blister under his bronze feet,
lie blood-hot slain on his double-edged sword,
cling to his smoldering sash
as he turns the terror of supernovae in his hand.

You there, with the shook-foil eyes.
Let me fall at the base of those lampstands,
light-headed from the simmering oil.
I won't even mention your name—
just dread you for a moment,
the waterfalls of your voice flooding my lungs
until you drop your stars and reach down.

Outside Delta, Utah

Off the Loneliest Road in America
a cottonwood quaked with a hundred pairs of shoes:
Adidas and Nikes slung by their strings,
salt-stained loafers and steel-toe boots,
Velcro Toy Story sandals, and—ah!—
so many ravishing Crocs departed all too soon.

The bone branches squeaked in the wind.
*Go to them. Learn of the things
that will soon take place.* I rubbed the gritty suede
of a 90s Birk, the oils of feet past rising
like incense. Could there be anything truer
than a tree of ten thousand miles walked?
Surely I would find the Alpha and Omega
in the gauzy, worn end of a Saucony lace.

I stuck my head in the heels. An All-Star's tongue
lolled over a leaf. *Be us,* he drawled. *Still in the twigs.
Warshed in the dust in the presence of God.*

I didn't believe a word. Hang still in the dust in 107
with thirty-three wars going on? There was a green
chile burrito getting cold on the dashboard
and farther west, I bet, bristlecones
born on the day of the Lord waiting for me,
wagging their evergreen tongues.

Ephesus

I was in love with God for one afternoon.
Twenty, alone on a beach, I dropped rocks
by the edge and watched the ocean wash
gray into blue, brown into red. An hour
of my crunching steps, the clack of pebbles,
the water's rippling response. Never mind
invisibility. We were the only ones, and I
so intoxicating—sand-blown hair,
denim cut-offs, no reason to believe
anyone's faith could dissolve. My prayers
were as certain as the stones I threw,
the answers as sure as the cove's blue floor.

Smyrna

No persecution in my leafy town,
so I turn myself over to my own hands,
forge iron bars, toss just enough fat
to train the lions for ravaging.

I rope myself to the stake.
Whom do I trust in the night?
My creator or wikis on cancerous moles?
The cords cut in. Do I dare breathe,
sing praise? Forgive the prick
who tailed me all the way home?

I could save some of my life
burning incense to the emperor of default.
He's capitulation, the whole day in bed.
He's rage's reward, the ice cream prayer,
the four hours of the Weather Channel
chasing tornadoes of my dread.

But I can never recant, even as fangs flash
and paws fling up the dust.
There's something about the smell
of bay laurel I can never leave behind—
lemons skimming a pitcher of water,
new rain on the mountains, the open-armed
aroma of plucked leaves woven together
and pressed to my exhausted head.

Pergamum

In the end, of course,
it was just

between us.
You held a flake

to my lips—
honey in hoarfrost.

And the stone
you pressed in my palm,

a magnolia bud
stippled with stars.

But my new name
was like nothing

created or spoken.
More elemental

than molecules
of wind, the inscription

of your breath.
This too I took

at the beginning
of my death

and held
beneath my tongue.

Thyatira

When you travel on business,
your spirit must take leave.

Suspended in the clouds
over Tokyo, you touch

the phone pic of your children
then wipe them away

like words on a whiteboard.
Your body does its job:

neon cocktails, hands under hems
in hostess bars.

You rip into a $250 steak
like it's a Little League hot dog,

trade jabs with your boss.
But still, projections look bleak.

Three years till the first starts college,
and you've amassed nothing

but the pulsing in your head,
hung over in the boardroom

as the morning star rises.
Your wife meets the bus after school

an ocean away, and—God forgive you—
as her face rises in your memory

you shove it back down, bind it
in layers of silk.

Sardis

She sprays the nursery toys with water and bleach,
erasing snot and drool from stacking rings,
wiping board books crimped by toddlers' teeth.
The congregation mingles in the wings.

The morning's Danish and donut halves go stale.
She wants to curl in the berbered corner to doze
but needs to dump and scour the diaper pail
before the second service fills the rows.

She dares to bow in the blocks to say a prayer
for the hands that will clutch these rattles and dolls,
but that woman with implants and highlit hair
nudges her friend and snickers down the hall.

Now whether to scrub the carpet's spit-up stains.
If it's even possible to strengthen what remains.

Philadelphia

Warning: In Case of Rapture,
This Car Will Be Unmanned

One day he would vaporize me through the windshield,
allow my Corolla to plow into the Goths

smoking on the street corner as I blasted off.
No way to save the screaming smudges down there.

Persecution was *Charles Darwin* on the bio study guide.
Depeche Mode. The Mapplethorpe exhibit in LA.

I had to tell myself that heaven would be so much better
than driving down Pacific Coast Highway,

peaches on the passenger seat, salt wind on my neck.
I would tan till lunch then realize I hadn't thought

of him once. Was I keeping watch? Would I be ready
if he sucked me from the sand? I would turn on my back

and swear to keep my word when I had nothing
to say, nothing to be saved from but a hell I couldn't see.

I held fast to an open door or, rather, the space
it left behind, driving home with coconut oil on my skin,

the sun in the mirrors, the uneasy hope of the saved.

Laodicea

Paul says your love has been poured
into my heart, which by heart
he means soul, which by soul
I mean belly.

But bile eddies there,
the acid I've thrown
in the faces of my beloveds
always trickling back.

You stand at the door and knock,
the quake before vomit.
Tightened throat, thudding ears.
Then the body's sudden liquefaction.

If I open, ignite me. Burn me clean
or just freeze me into rest.
Or swallow me and spit me out
so I can stagger back to you.

The Great Throne

Rabbi, I'm losing you in all these robes,
like a kid tunneling through a department store rack,
pummeled by grown-up fabric.

The rainbow anchors its feet like a guard.
If you're the one I used to know,
sand in your hair and leper skin

under your nails, you wouldn't barricade yourself
with torches, light your face carnelian
like a haunted house clown. Holy

is sensing a woman's touch through your hem,
not bulldozing souls with thunder.
You don't need thousands of unblinking eyes

staring you down over a great glass sea
when the fish of Galilee peer at your calloused feet
skimming the water like sunlight.

Jasper

If God is made of jasper and carnelian
then I should wear him on my throat and wrists
where my own blood can beat against the shine
of deity chucked from speckled schist.

St. John envisioned gems as blazing drops
of holiness. He shuddered, wept, and fell.
When I type jasper into Google Shop
I find it strung with silver plated shells

or hung with dragonflies on leather cords.
Or find no stone but a laminated square
where *Twilight*'s brooding Jasper Hale can bore
a hole into a tween with his smoky stare

so she can gaze down at her chest each day,
and sighing, turn him upside down and pray.

Our Sins under a Glass Sea

Jesus wanted to shout *damn it to hell!*
when he dropped the jar of mayonnaise,
the *words* not a temptation as much as succumbing
to a belief in personal justice,
cursing a world that dare exist
without intact jars and the right to fork
modified food starch through tuna on demand.
Instead, he mended the glass outside
of time and space, invited the twenty-four elders
with emerald butter knives to spread their riches
on slices of bread. He smirked at the bespattered
refrigerator door, breathed *YHWH*
as he hunkered over the slimy shards
with a roll of paper towels. His knuckles scraped
the floor as he scrubbed oil from the grout,
lightning flashing in the dustpan by his side.

The Scroll and the Seven Seals

John wept when no one would break the seal. All of God's voices
and mountains and bodies and planets rolled up in a sheepskin—so
close! The wax globs glowed in the jasper. The beasts snuffled and
shuffled their hooves, their thousands of black eyes blinking. A bit
awkward, John's blubbering under the emerald rainbow while the
twenty-four elders looked down at their robes. The angel didn't
mean to string him along. And truth is, I wanted to know those
secrets, too. Touch some God particles, hear the trumpet, figure
out just how Jesus would clean up the pedophiles and wars. But
not enough to weep. Those thunderclaps would have sent my kids
flying to my bed. That's what I wanted—yesterday's hot breath of
my daughter on my cheek. The gray cat I rescued in fifth grade,
tail whipping like this ghastly lion's. And these seven torches of the
spirit—could I think of anything but the college bonfires where we
lifted our hands and sang? Our praise was incense, we chorused,
faces lit carnelian. We prayed for graduate degrees and engagement
rings when we knew full well they were coming, our futures like the
throne's great glass sea. Oh, heaven, we pleaded, come down to us
soon, oh heaven, meant for anyone but us.

LOCUSTS
ON
THE
EARTH

The First Horse of the Apocalypse

You were born a swath of frost
in the clover, nudged up
on icicle legs. Now you cut

through men like a derecho,
sulfur and Sodom in your nostrils,
entrails winding your hooves.

I am trying to believe that God
doesn't will destruction, that out of love
he allows our terrible freedoms

to gallop across the globe.
The arrows tremble in your shoulders.
I pull them out, hum softly

and stroke your heaving flanks,
even if your rider presses his sword to my neck,
even if the book says I'm too late.

The Second Horseman Speaks

Child, I will peel the glow stars
from your ceiling, silence the cicadas

and wake you from the peace
you never knew you had.

Mother will find the lump.
Father will leave when her last hair falls.

Third grade will fight to keep you
another year, and when the bike chain snaps

on the other side of town, the sun spilling
its blood on your neck, you will know

just how alone you are.

This was not the job I wanted.
God spoke, and the red horse came charging.

*Remove peace from the earth
so that people will slay one another.*

I don't know how to start a border skirmish
or stir up rebels in Luxembourg.

But a small soul can be wrenched
from its maker, destruction so easy to pursue.

Cover your head with your pillow, child.
I am starting with you.

A Road Worker Confronts the Third Horseman of the Apocalypse

Then I heard . . . a voice among the four living creatures,
saying, "Two pounds of wheat for a day's wages. . . ."

That scale in your hand swinging
a couple loaves of Wonder
comes out to nine and a half hours
of banging hot mix into potholes
as my lungs fill with the exhaust
of people skipping town for good.

Of course we can't let our kids starve.
My wife scrubs hospital toilets
as her stomach growls for dead people's
half-eaten Jell-O. Her paycheck will cover
one jar of peanut butter our boys
will attack with clanging spoons.

But you, soldier, with your steady job
of prophecy, eating among thousand-eyed
eagles and lions. One man can change things,
you know. If you really cared about God's love
you'd go back and kick over some tables.
Jesus did something like that.

But hey, slow down! You're making it all blow away.
You think I'm too proud to chase after some crusts?
Hell, no, cowboy. And don't you dare
peel the bread off that chain-link fence.
My body may be broken,
but I'll be damned if I let it die.

The Fourth Horseman of the Apocalypse

You say you will never forsake us
then send a horse the color of decaying flesh
to wipe out a fourth of the earth.

God does not will woe, the pastor says. Disaster unfolds
from our own misdeeds. We sing, lift hands.
The drummer kicks out mercy and grace.

But I still see the horse trampling the bloated faces
once knit in their mothers' wombs,
coyotes gnawing on bones in brown pastures.

Jesus, you slid screaming from a birth canal,
kissed leprous flesh and bantered with whores.
Now you're lounging among gemstones

while viruses shut down newborn organs
and ashes coat the treads of our shoes.
You don't have to end it this way.

But even if you don't, even if this slaughter
is just another symbol of our exodus
from your love,

why invent a cadaverous horse
to instruct us, why sharpen more swords,
why, bloodied lamb, even break the seal?

Souls Beneath the Altar

They cried out with a loud voice, "O Sovereign Lord,
holy and true, how long before you will judge and
avenge our blood on those who dwell on the earth?"

God, I am so close to you now
I can hold your hem to my face
and watch the incense
settle in the scars on your feet.

You tell me to wait
on my rage, put on my white robe
and be still. I had thought I wanted
to hide in your spun silk

and ignore the blistering world.
But the persecutors
pummeled a teenager
digging a well, threw gasoline

and matches in a prayer room
and flung me to the floor
as I sang.
They sliced my throat,

and as I strangled my last
breath, I saw the man
who held my neck with one hand
yank a naked child by the hair

with the other. Are you telling me
he knew not what he did?
Must he wake again and again
to wrap himself in the sun?

I am so close to you now
I can hold your hem to my face.
I am so close to you I must tell you
you are wrong.

A Quick Interpretation of the Sixth Seal

The sun turning to sackcloth
means *nothing to see here;*
all the sheeted corpses look the same.

The moon surging with blood
equals the deaths your butterfly wings
effected while you slept.

And the stars sizzling at your feet
like Epsom salts is his way of saying
you've lost your chances

with time and space.
The sky will snap closed like a scroll,
and you will be left

with the black hole of God
as you hide in the small breathing spaces
of fallen mountains,

which means he'll know
just where to look
before wrenching you back to his chest.

On the Eve of the End of the World

DECEMBER 20, 2012

Some said the angels would pin back
the four winds of the earth
and toss us our white robes,
but the porch chairs are still tumbling
around the patio, and I haven't ascended
from the couch.

I half-doze to freezing rain
rattling like the jade necklaces of Mayans
who knew nothing of Christ
when they lay down their time,
nothing of the shining 144K.
I'll find some Mayans in the multitude

a thousand years later and tease
about the week NASA fielded tearful calls
and Facebook exploded with doomsday memes—
the same week armed men and drones
killed children in schoolrooms
and veins popped at the edge

of a fiscal cliff. The first snow
of the winter hit, too, I'll tell them.
It was all I could see out the window
when I pulled a blanket to my chin
and, thank God,
slept through the end of the age.

The Mark of the Lamb

Meanwhile, the 144,000 received the mark of the lamb,
a paw print of glitter on their foreheads.

His voice washed over them like a river lit with silt.
Harps rolled out the thickest, goldest arpeggios.

We've been instructed to want a Baz Luhrmann afterlife,
not the subtle, oaky undertones of Christ in the wilderness,

women spilling hair on his feet. But when I died,
I turned away from the light. Walk toward my face,

he said. Quiet, thorn-pocked, creased with the desert.
Reflections of unthrown stones in his eyes.

The Sun Shall Not Strike Them

You made her choke until she vomited.
    Where does her help come from?

She forgave because Jesus said 70 times,
    and this was only 21.

So that Sunday you preached 70 times 7,
    and she slid down the pew like a shadow.

Why are you crying? You asked that night.
    You would neither slumber nor sleep.

She was nine, trying to count in her head:
    470, 469 more. . .then I can get mad?

Stop crying, you hissed.
    But the floor's cold. You're smushing me.

You brought a blanket. You kept her from evil.
    She forgave to 435.

Some nights she clutched her stomach,
    waiting. Some nights you let her

keep her nightgown on. *Thank you,* she told you.
    I love you. 422.

She whimpered that your zipper
    cinched her skin,

when you actually unzipped her,
    from that time forth and forevermore,

a life of marbles and times tables
    and Etch-a-Sketch sand spilling out

as she held nothing together,
    no whole she knew worth saving.

She lifted her eyes, fixed them
    on the bathroom's corner tile to number 409.

Even now, decades later, she says she could have
    brought it on herself. *No!* I snap,

and find myself thinking of serrated knives
    doing things I've never imagined.

My kids sit in the school lunchroom now
    with the ripped and ridiculed—

like how you told her, at 397,
    next time bathe down there.

Which girl picking listlessly at chips
    will be asked to guide her torturer

to the right groaning spot,
    Which boy will fall asleep coloring

while keeping watch in the moon by night?
    Which will not be believed?

One day, I assure her, there will be no more
    suffering, no more tears.

You took her to 382. You kept your life.
    When will your crying begin?

There Was Silence in Heaven for Half an Hour

—at a writing retreat

The full inhalation
before the coming of the kingdom.

Pencils scuttling over legal pads,
hands whispering in beards.

Friend, I know the sound
of your water bottle flipping open.

Brother, I've memorized
your bare feet on wooden floors.

One of you runs a bath upstairs,
a year of sorrows draining down.

One of you spreads out a manuscript,
pages setting sail in your fingers.

The lake sobs on the shore.
Rain perpendiculars the panes,

Beloved, and you stretch
your knuckles to the ceiling.

The golden censer of thunder
shudders just above the shingles.

We pass around a bowl of candy,
holding each other's breath.

The Seventh Seal

You pray and get blood and hail
in return. Send up incense

only for angels to hurl embers
back down on your head.

The light of Wormwood
torches your face—

you feel the rush
of a child whose mother

looks him warm in the eye
while waving a wooden spoon.

One day love and judgment
will click. Now a poison star

splashes a third of the rivers
on Earth. You should want God

to batter and consume. You cup
the murk, feel your vessels burn.

Jesus took the vinegar
as the sky turned black—his last taste

so bitter, so bitten with bad fruit,
it ripped his spirit clean out.

Locusts on the Earth

All that grace wasn't working
anymore, the Kinkade prints

and purpose-driven songs,
kids star-charting memorized verses.

He needed something big, something
like a horse with an exoskeleton

and a supermodel's hair.
Smoke, breastplates, crowns.

The people clawed the walls of ambulances.
They writhed in hospital hallways

until released back to parking lots
shrilling with yellow-gauze wings.

I thought it a little much, scorpion tails
shooting people in grocery aisles,

knocking them down at bus stops
until they locked themselves inside,

shivering as the hissing shook their windows.
But what did I know? Some of them

began to sing. Some of them collapsed
in prayer to their tormenter.

After five months of venom in their veins,
some of them fell paralyzed in love.

Maybe an Idol

The hot rotten eggs of my destruction,
locust stingers jouncing in my skin like arrows:

fantasies of stasis.

I cannot acquiesce to the grooves
above my lip. I massage them with serum

from a silver tube, comb Revlon Golden Brown
through my roots. Dye stipples my hands

like tar spots on maple leaves.
Sometimes I catch a flash of fifteen in the mirror:

Sponge rollers, aqua eyes, skirt tiered
with fuchsia lace. Dread trembles in my lips.

We want so few of our idols.

At night, my back hurts like labor.
I no longer turn, but reverse in my bed,

crown at the footboard. I wake to forget,
my hair still damp with hope,

dog wheezing in my ear
like wind through a tent flap.

My husband caresses my cracked feet
He doesn't know where I've gone.

I curl my spine against his shins, forgiven.

The Angel and the Little Scroll

sweet in my mouth but bitter

You've got a jumbo rainbow
Over your head and a sun
for a face like something
from My Little Pony.
We're finally finished
with sulfur and plagues.
Time to curl up with Jesus!
But then you pop open the thunder
and roar, straddling earth
and sea as if to say, not so fast—
you might be drowned.
Or baptized again.
God can throw down a raven
or dove. Who's to say?
But what a shimmer in your palm,
a scroll like a golden
Fruit Roll-Up. You shrug
and hold it out to me.
Your stomach's gonna kill,
you say. But I don't care.
God's got a recipe.
Once I start unfurling
and chewing those words,
I just can't stop.

The Witness

He lay dead in the street for three and a half days,
skin undulating with flies. His payment for pouring fire
on the holdouts. From the soul-cloud he watched

the unbelievers bumping and grinding in celebration.
Exchanging their oxy and smack. In life
he could never confess he didn't blame them

for resisting a *god* who sunk his fingers into leprous flesh.
Who whispered to whores. Who rolled out of a cave—
did he? could he?—demanding kisses and fists.

Until the witnesses themselves rose up to join him.
Until the earth knocked down seven thousand
with falling stones, and nobody knew what to think.

Michael and the Dragon

This lizard did not deserve a Hollywood slaying—
septuple headlock and sword in the heart,
tail lopped off only to regenerate

in one of John's fitful island nights.
Michael just gave the nod,
and the angels flickered around the beast

like gypsy moths. Dragon snorted. *Seriously?*
Burped sulfur. Thrashed. But they hung
from his horns as his minions slithered off

like oil-slick feathers. Michael yanked
his scales one by one, at first a pesky itch
until the full air of heaven hit

like gold gravel on the skin.
The shrill testimonial songs of the saved
raked over the raw surface.

Earth lurched for him. Even crying hurt.
He wrapped his tail around himself
and like a plucked chicken dropped.

The Woman and the Dragon

After the baby ripped a lightning bolt in her perineum,
the dragon drooling from his seven heads while awaiting
his first bite, she could only think, *then what the hell
was all that for?* Soon the placenta pulsed out, the reptile
whipped down a few thousand stars with his tail,
and the curdle-skinned boy screamed and rooted for her breast.
Can we just rest a minute before we die?

You never remember the pain, her mother once said
after screaming out a seventh sibling. She knew a mother's lie
when she heard one. When God whisked the baby
from the dragon's jaws and sent her off to the wilderness,
she collapsed under a sycamore and held the blood
between her legs. *Thank God,* she thought, scanning the trees.
Thank God there are no men here.

The Antichrist at the Mall

Who wouldn't marvel at a leopard
with seven heads, crowns dangling from his horns
like rhinestone belts?

He stops you at every kiosk.
Look into my lion's mouth.
Hold my grizzly paws to your cheek.

You can't move around him.
He sprawls into the walkway,
and you sink into his flanks.

I look beautiful on you, he purrs,
as hanging video screens lurch with teens
and pretzels rise in their ovens.

Darling, *your god took off awhile ago*
like a balloon through the skylights.
I am available today only.

One easy payment even you can afford.

The Mark of the Beast

Whatever you do, mom tells me at bedtime,
don't let a creature put a mark on your head.
I'll probably be long dead and gone.

There is no such thing as far, as future.
I lie under an avalanche of stuffed animals,
sick over kickball in the morning.

Probably when the years start with twenty,
she says. *That* then. When I will ride the monorail
in my pigtails and silver jumpsuit,

the sky and its ships sinking closer.
A Blue Meanie or Snuffleupagus
hurtling toward me with a librarian's stamp.

When he comes, just duck and pray to Jesus.
I try that most days, when the ball
flies toward my left-field hiding place,

my teammates throwing down their caps.
Our Father who art in heaven,
please let it go the other way

before I clasp the air and trip, drop it
between my pencil legs, or face another
horrible end I can't predict.

The Winepress of Wrath

Nicked, sickle-swept,
bobbling with the other souls
   in a juice-stained basket.
How will I be saved?

   We tremble in the vat.
The ball of his foot descends
   with the thrill and terror
of a solar eclipse.

   It's one of the stories
I've trimmed from my Bible,
   now a gathering of thin, white petals
fragrant with olive blossoms.

   But no time to waste seething
at the apparitions of Jesus
   Ginsuing iron blades in the clouds.
I can roll out of here,

   dry up in defense, or—
if he's still game—
   become his first miracle
of wine.

En Route, Tikrit

The teenager in a soccer jersey, tossed on a salvage bed like scrap
    metal,
buries his face in the red T-shirt of a man who's tucked his head
in the plaid armpit of another, the whole male village a swath of
    rumbling cotton
murmuring *Shit,* and *Jesus help us,* sharing their last communion of
    piss
in a truck snuffling like a horned beast in the desert. Just yesterday
he saw his sister raped and pledged to take charge of the world.
Now he clings to a man's waist, vomits and whispers psalms,
dizzy with visions of angels on fire tightening their golden sashes.
He feels their silk on his face, and when they lift their golden bowls
    of wrath,
says, *Come on, dammit. Pour it down. C'mon, let it sizzle this time.*

The Seven Bowls of God's Wrath

I.

I bowed before the beast.
It was all I knew how to do.
Even though the gravel
(Big-Bang blasted!)
imbedded my knees
I knelt till my skin grew over.

II.

Because I did not believe
the sea turned to blood.
I could have held on
wrangled with God on the cold cliffs
gulls screeching
but it was easier to open my hands
and slip in

III.

Look, there is still only blood
to drink   bubbling
from the springs.
They're bottling it now,
my face on the label.
BOGO the rest of the week.

IV.

I will not repent,
even as the sunflames
lurch down on me,
I will clench them
like reins, ride his anger
all the way to the pit
of his heart

V.

It is so dark now,
I can't even see the sores.
They sting even more
when I am alone
no bodies to block the wind.
I want to be alone.

VI.

Spots in my eyes
flickered face
wet leaping
tongue zipping
tadpoles in my hair
If I open my mouth

They can speak for me, sure
I will take their nightsong
I have nothing better to say.

VII.

Overpasses down,
islands sunk,
hundred-pound hailstones
cannon-balled to the gut.
Is this all you've got, God?
I'm over here,
perched on the wreckage
of the Grand Avenue bridge.
Oh, fire now?
If I just wave my arms,
I know you'll wrench me out.
But I'm ready to run.

The Great Harlot Takes a Selfie

She smolders for the reverse camera,
lipstick feathered from servicing
a few more kings of the earth.

But she knows a filter that will douse
her purple and scarlet dress with light,
shine up her old pearls like the teeth of seraphim.

If she holds the golden cup too high,
a few abominations will lap at the rim.
So she tips it just outside the frame

for a rosy glow of blood, allows a point
of the beast's horn to flirt in the corner
like a quarter-inch hint of cleavage.

So much outrage these days—
Kardashian's ass, decapitated bodies
in trenches. *I'm going for something more. . .*

something less *defined.* Software won't block her.
She will fill your feed with gauzy edges
of desire. Every time you go looking

for Jesus, you will fall into her folds.
You will scroll and refresh, scroll and refresh,
forgetting what you were trying to find.

The Babylon in My Body

In one hour, all this wealth has been laid waste.
The cinnamon and myrrh under my skin
sizzle with fever. Flute players suffocate,
knock their metal against my bones.

Love me, world, I've moaned all along.
Lie with me, take body shots among my pearls.
The ships unload my emeralds of words.
My laughter unrolls like silk.

And now just the smoldering edges
of a soul once wrought with stars.
All my delicacies and splendor lost, the vultures
whisking my nerves with their ragged songs.

The End of Babylon

The smoke of her destruction
goes up forever and ever,
    hallelujah.

The ashes of her spent sex
seem to whirl from the cup
on the Dunkin' Donuts sign—

though actually farther off,
as fires typically are,
    praise the Lord.

They say she smolders behind
the broken-window clinic
the next town over—
    rejoice!—

tattered white skirts
surrendering to the sky,
dirty lace unraveling.

March toward New Jerusalem.
Don't turn back to the vapors
snaking behind us
like exhaust from a dryer.

Jasper walls ahead.
Emerald, lapis lazuli.

Remember the laundry days,
I say, and for a flash
want a basketful of warm towels,
Bounce sheets mingled with socks,

a host of steaming sins,
    hallelujah.

AND THEY SANG A NEW SONG

The Rider on a White Horse

Last week a neighborhood
eighth-grader shot himself.

Here's the space
between joint and marrow:

before prayer—before the bore
of mourning—gossip lit and rippled

through me like the neon frenzy
of the Vegas strip. You tell me

I'm only human. That's why the warrior
packed a winepress and rod.

Drugs, girl, gay, depressed?
Note, gun case, temple, mouth?

Christ charges in on a horse,
the blood on his dipped robe

his own. He punches at the seams,
billows parachute-style

over the armed borders of my thoughts.
And when I crawl out swinging,

he lets go the muscled flanks
like whitecaps. I can see just

flame, linen, diadem.
Pain, love, pain.

Double-Edged Sword

Fear not the fear mongers
and their thorn-crowned ax murderer

charging the crowd on a white horse,
wild-eyed for commies and gays.

Christ comes after you with nothing more
than a word in his mouth:

just a double-edged marrow
splitter, knife handle

jostling in his jaws. *Sell it all.*
Despise your children. Gouge your eye

and ankle-hack. Pulverize a camel
through the needle's blistering chink.

You bones. You shriveled figs.
You knockabout whitewashed hearts.

Did he ever know you?
You hope to God to lose your life.

Shivering in the splendor of a lily,
you bleed.

A Premillennialist, Amillennialist, and Postmillennialist Walk Into a Bar

Man to man, says the premillennialist to the postmillennialist.
If Jesus were to return today,
do you know where you would go?

I'm good, Post smiles, and raises his beer.
We'll all turn out just fine.

The amillennialist sighs and knocks one back.
Christ sure has his work cut out.

Hell—I mean, heck—yeah! Premil pumps his fist.
Can't wait to see the look on the devil's face
when he locks him to that chain!

Chain? Post says.
Satan and I were just serving soup
to the poor. I knew he'd come around.

Oh, he's locked up all right, says Amil.
Been locked up for two thousand years.

Premil stares. *You sure you're saved?*

Kirk Cameron imbecile! Amil yells.
Godless liberal! wails Premil.
(Just so you know, I'm not drunk.)

Hey, Post says. *One day we'll all look back
on this and laugh.*

Oh yeah? says Premil, raising an eyebrow.
When?

The Book of the Dead

And if it contains the entire life record of all people,
how much time would it take to read it?
    —Augustine, *City of God*

Imagine the longest open mic reading in the world,
angels droning out deeds and misdeeds
in—Lord have mercy!—poet voice.

Henrietta Blackwell. . .stole. . . a dairy cow? In 1663?

Feng Lee threw a rock. At a city bus.
The dates. . . (dramatic hand reach) *are numerous.*

The heavenly host don't know when or whether
to applaud. After each name? Nation? Dirty look
catalogued in the billions of dirty looks?
And the murders, rapes, and burning cities:
how many mournful *hm*'s and sighs can they muster?

Worst of all, the angel who goes over his allotted time
in order to read *just one more* piece, something he threw together
on the spot (he says this proudly!) while the others were up.

It is a story of an Ethiopian boy in 340 AD
who jumped into a river to save a girl
after beating another girl within an inch.

So is he in or is he out? The other angels ask,
but the reader details every grain of sand
on the shore, every antenna of every insect
crawling on the boy's skin as the sun filtered
through elliptical leaves to light the filaments of his hair.
And when the boy leapt toward the flailing arms
and hung suspended over the water *as if all time stopped,*
even the multitudinous planets in their monumental orbits,
the angels begin joggling their knees, ratting their hems,
laying their heads on their arms and delivering the sighs
that more considerate, socially aware angels would interpret
as clues to shut up and sit down already.

Some members of the audience shake out their wings
and stand up. Others converse.
Gabriel reaches for the switch on the cappuccino machine
but Jesus grabs his arm.

Not yet, he says, staring up front. *I want to hear this one.*

The Book of Life

Jesus saunters up to the mic,
opens the book, and stares at the audience.

Silence. Exactly how narrow *was* this road?

Too many to list, he says, and slams it closed.
Come on, guys.

Let's get the hell out of here.

The Marriage Supper

Ours tumbled from a bag
onto a hotel bed at one in the morning.

Finally safe from the jangles of laughter,
divorced parents' glares,

and one hundred bobby pins
woven against my scalp,

we had checked hasty sex off the list
and driven our rental Taurus

through Taco Bell. We had not eaten
in sixteen hours.

I was not radiant. Dressed in sweats
and Mexi-melt wrappers, I licked hot sauce

from the webs of my fingers,
pinched shredded cheese and dozed off

from our salty consummation.
Twenty-one years later,

we check into our room
with dinner and a show already behind us.

We still have hours to celebrate.
I let a few grays fall over my negligee

and unseal a box of cheap chocolates.
No hurry—

the chart shows plenty of caramels left,
and the bride has made herself ready.

And They Sang a New Song

God is not the author of confusion.
There's a way to hear the myriads sing
when you lie addled on your couch.
Wood chippers: *Worthy is the lamb.*
Diesel engines: *Weep no more.*
Don't say it isn't beautiful.
Everything above, on, and under.
Garters, voles and fruit bats
hallowing your yard with slither and gnaw.

Hallow my yard with slither and gnaw,
all you garters and voles and fruit bats.
Everything above, under, and on!
Don't say it isn't beautiful,
diesel engines. Weep no more,
O wood chippers. Worthy is your lamb.
When I lie addled in this church,
there's a way to make the myriads sing
with you, God. Stay. Author my confusion.

New Jerusalem

Alpha, Omega: it makes no difference.
The heavenly city of God has come down.

He makes his dwelling place
in the muddy corner of your garage,

the oncologist's office,
the space between paper and pen.

Run your fingers along the foundation walls
studded with onyx and topaz.

Bask in the jasper.
Hear the gate-squeak of pearl on gold.

Pain and tears will pass away,
but for now he bedazzles

your blisters and tissue,
saline and nerve,

somehow—do you believe it?—
the neck of a kneeling man

about to lose his head to the sand.
He prays for water, just one last

drink. The sword lifts,
then springs bubble up in the dark.

The River of Life

At the end of it all, I find you on the street.
That you? I ask.
Yes, you too?
We touch His name on our foreheads.
Well.

You take my hand, but our fingers
slip like feathers.
No longer given in marriage, you say.
Oh, I smile. *Right.*

We watch the river tumble
through fruit-heavy trees.
So clear, I say, *like those beads
from the craft store.*
Or more like His spit, you laugh.
Crafts. Stores. A world smaller than a leaf.

Remember that river we crossed with the kids?
You snap your fingers. *The kids!*
At Glacier, a footbridge, no rails.
You carried them over, and I closed my eyes.

I remind you that a woman fell
from that bridge the next day. *But now—*
I peer at you sideways—*no death.*

Yes. I think that's her now, crossing.
Where?

By His face.

Where is His face?

You spread your arms wide. *Can't you see?*

Coming Soon

I did not ask to be created,
yet here I wait for my creator to return.

Backspacing into a garden
before serpents unspooled from trees,

before I positioned ficus leaves
around my hips.

Naked and unafraid: I forgot
what that was like.

Soon and very soon, we sing.
Jesus will soon take place.

Don't guess the hour—
but everybody seems to find him:

his face imprinted on slices of toast,
breath in the form of gold dust on a scarf.

I doubt, love, need, forget.
But come and get me, thief.

Scramble. Cut your arms and legs
through the fog like blades

of the bright morning star.

ACKNOWLEDGMENTS

Books & Culture: "The Angel Over Patmos," "The Mark of the Beast," "The Mark of the Lamb," "Pergamum"

The Christian Century: "Ephesus," "The Great Throne," "There Was Silence in Heaven for Half an Hour"

Cresset: "Patmos," "The Things That Must Soon Take Place"

Image: "The First Horse of the Apocalypse," "The Fourth Horseman of the Apocalypse," "A Quick Interpretation of the Sixth Seal"

Letters: "Philadelphia"

Perspectives: "Locusts on the Earth"

Relief: "The Angel and the Little Scroll," "The Seven Bowls of God's Wrath," "Vision of the Son of Man"

Rock & Sling: "Our Sins Under a Glass Sea"

Ruminate: "And They Sang a New Song," "The Babylon in My Body"

Windhover: "The Antichrist at the Mall," "Behold, He is Coming on the Clouds"

ABOUT PARACLETE PRESS

Who We Are

Paraclete Press is a publisher of books, recordings, and DVDs on Christian spirituality. Our publishing represents a full expression of Christian belief and practice—from Catholic to Evangelical, from Protestant to Orthodox.

We are the publishing arm of the Community of Jesus, an ecumenical monastic community in the Benedictine tradition. As such, we are uniquely positioned in the marketplace without connection to a large corporation and with informal relationships to many branches and denominations of faith.

What We Are Doing

PARACLETE PRESS BOOKS | Paraclete publishes books that show the richness and depth of what it means to be Christian. Although Benedictine spirituality is at the heart of who we are and all that we do, we publish books that reflect the Christian experience across many cultures, time periods, and houses of worship. We publish books that nourish the vibrant life of the church and its people.

We have several different series, including the bestselling Paraclete Essentials and Paraclete Giants series of classic texts in contemporary English; Voices from the Monastery—men and women monastics writing about living a spiritual life today; our award-winning Paraclete Poetry series as well as the Mount Tabor Books on the arts; bestselling gift books for children on the occasions of baptism and first communion; and the Active Prayer Series that brings creativity and liveliness to any life of prayer.

MOUNT TABOR BOOKS | Paraclete's newest series, Mount Tabor Books, focuses on the arts and literature as well as liturgical worship and spirituality, and was created in conjunction with the Mount Tabor Ecumenical Centre for Art and Spirituality in Barga, Italy.

PARACLETE RECORDINGS | From Gregorian chant to contemporary American choral works, our recordings celebrate the best of sacred choral music composed through the centuries that create a space for heaven and earth to intersect. Paraclete Recordings is the record label representing the internationally acclaimed choir Gloriæ Dei Cantores, praised for their "rapt and fathomless spiritual intensity" by *American Record Guide*; the Gloriæ Dei Cantores Schola, specializing in the study and performance of Gregorian chant; and the other instrumental artists of the Arts Empowering Life Foundation.

Paraclete Press is also privileged to be the exclusive North American distributor of the recordings of the Monastic Choir of St. Peter's Abbey in Solesmes, France, long considered to be a leading authority on Gregorian chant.

PARACLETE VIDEO | Our DVDs offer spiritual help, healing, and biblical guidance for a broad range of life issues including grief and loss, marriage, forgiveness, facing death, bullying, addictions, Alzheimer's, and spiritual formation.

Learn more about us at our website:
www.paracletepress.com or phone us
toll-free at 1.800.451.5006

SCAN
TO
READ
MORE

MORE PARACLETE POETRY

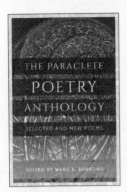

Paraclete Poetry Anthology
Mark S. Burrows, editor,
Foreword by Jon M. Sweeney
ISBN: 978-1-61261-906-4
$20.00 French flaps

This anthology spans the first ten years of the poetry series at Paraclete Press. Included are poems by Phyllis Tickle, Scott Cairns, Paul Mariani, Anna Kamieńska, Fr. John-Julian, SAID, Bonnie Thurston, Greg Miller, William Woolfitt, Rami Shapiro, Thomas Lynch, Paul Quenon, and Rainer Maria Rilke.

"Paraclete is a house firmly rooted in presenting and curating religious poetry as part of the verbal experience that, being couched more deeply in the aesthetic than the didactic, has deep resonance and potent significance for the shaping of the surrounding culture itself. It means the on-going giving away and sharing of God with humility through mystery."
—PHYLLIS TICKLE (1934–2015)

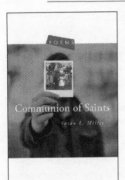

Communion of Saints
Susan L. Miller
ISBN: 978-1-61261-858-6
$18.00 Trade paper

Communion of Saints is a collection of poems that explores the saints of the church's history and contemporary persons who embody something of their charism. Three sections are arranged around the themes of the three theological virtues:

— Faith, portrayed as a source of strength in times of trial
— Hope, the darkest in the book, dealing with matters of the body's frailty, illness, social discrimination, and the search for a way to live within the constraints of society
— Love, offering a panoply of outward-looking characters who give to others in radical or personal ways

The volume ends with a cycle of Franciscan poems that offer a model for the Christian life, not simply in terms of individual moments but also as a complete life-cycle of practice and prayer.

Available from your local bookseller or through Paraclete Press:
www.paracletepress.com; 1-800-451-5006